If I had a flower

A FLORAL COLORING BOOK

An adult coloring book
containing 17 beautiful flowers and
floral designs to color. Designs including
skulls, floral turtles, mandalas and
many flowers

If I had a flower

A FLORAL COLORING BOOK

Have a question? Let us know
shawonbryant8718@gmail.com

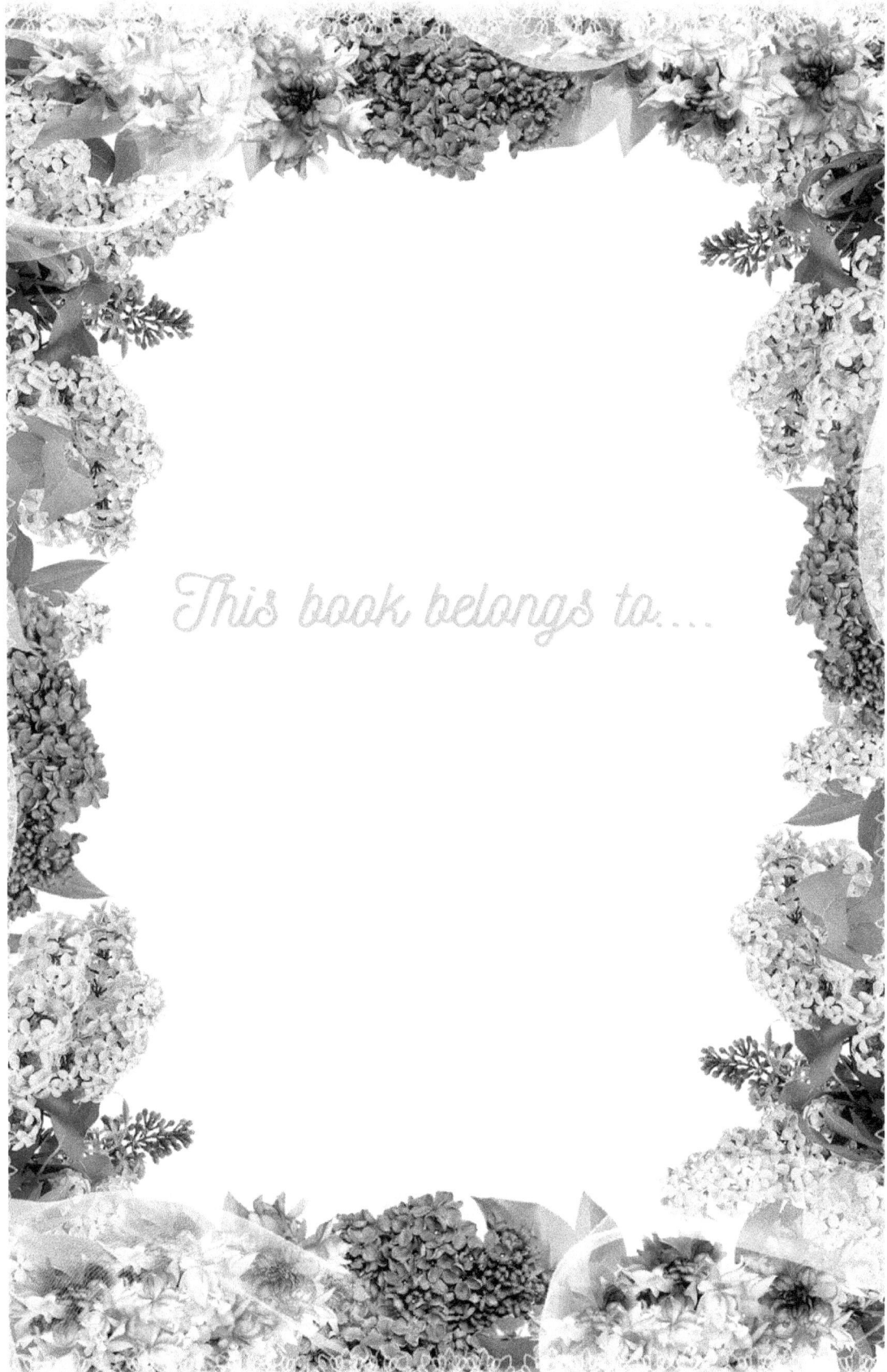

This book belongs to....

Beautiful Floral Mandala

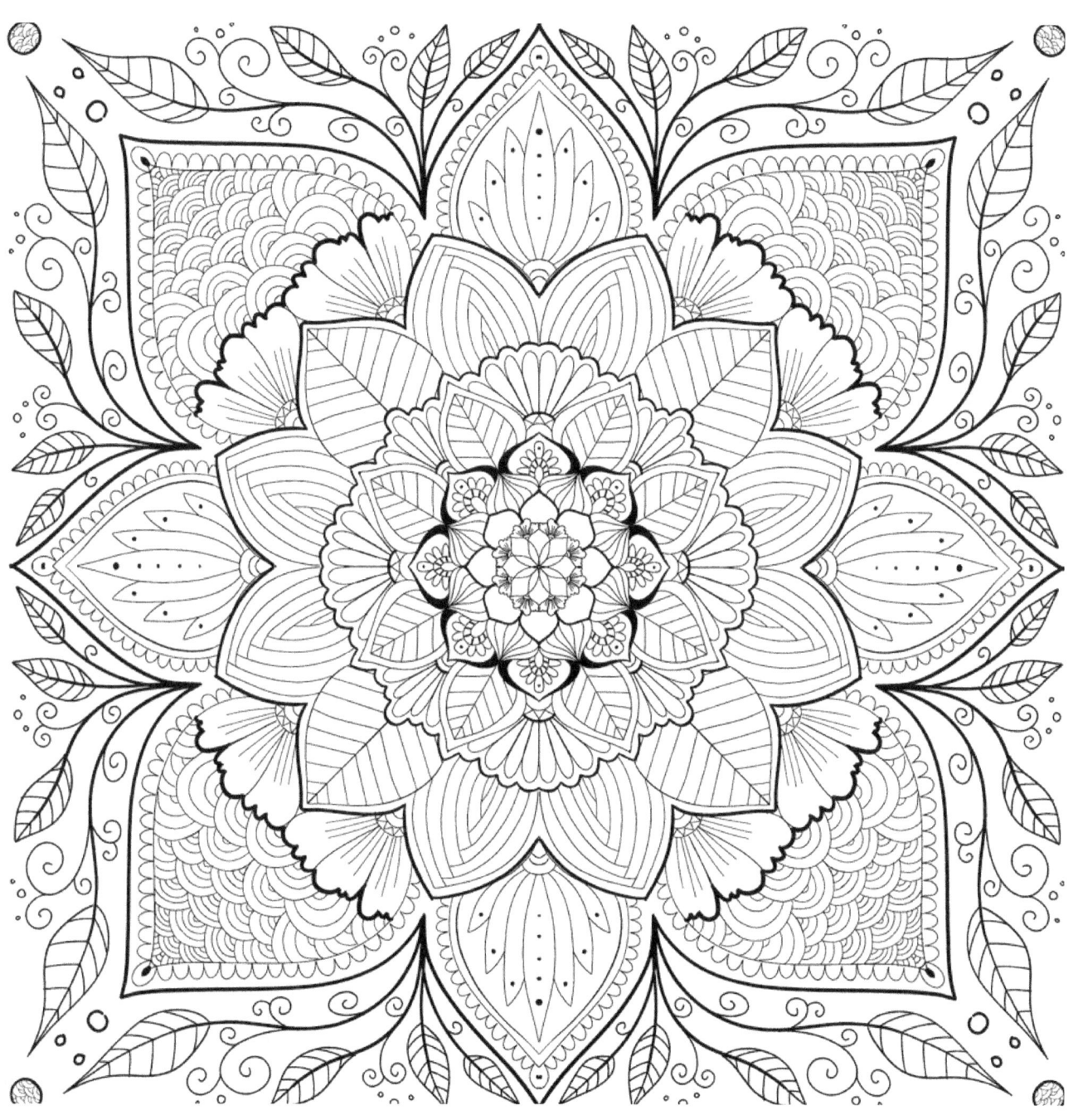

Roses

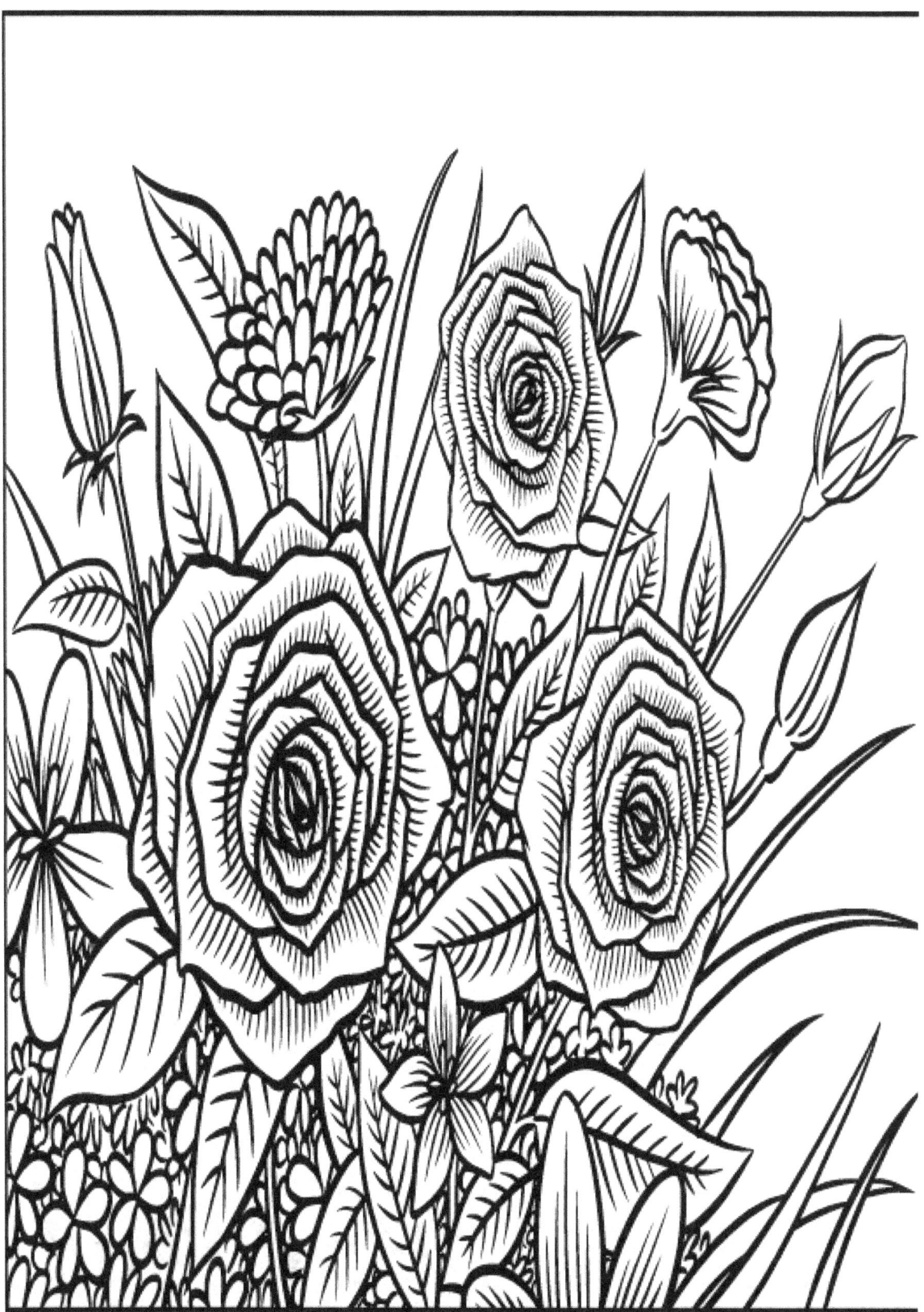

Floral Skull

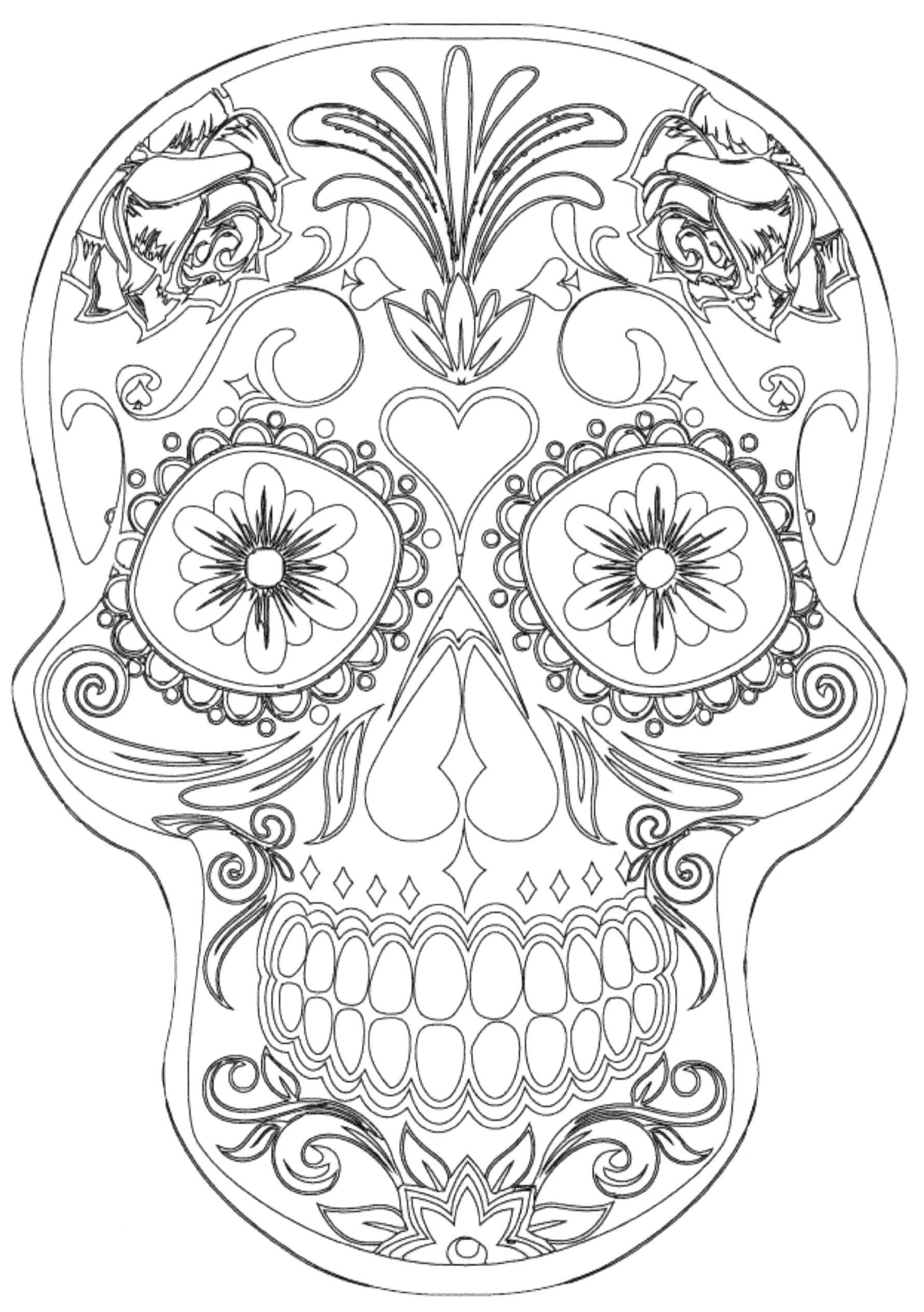

Floral Turtle

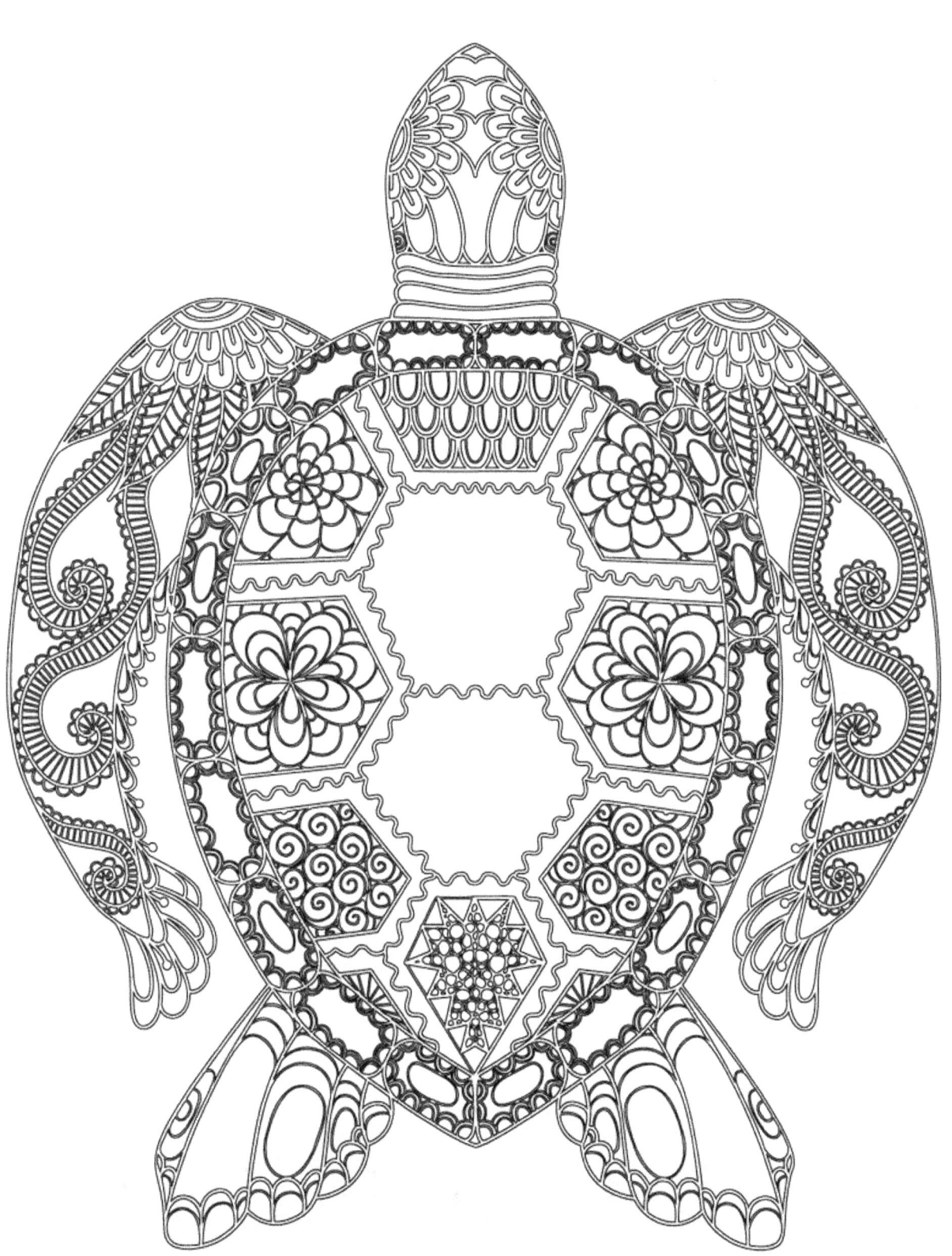

One Beautiful Rose

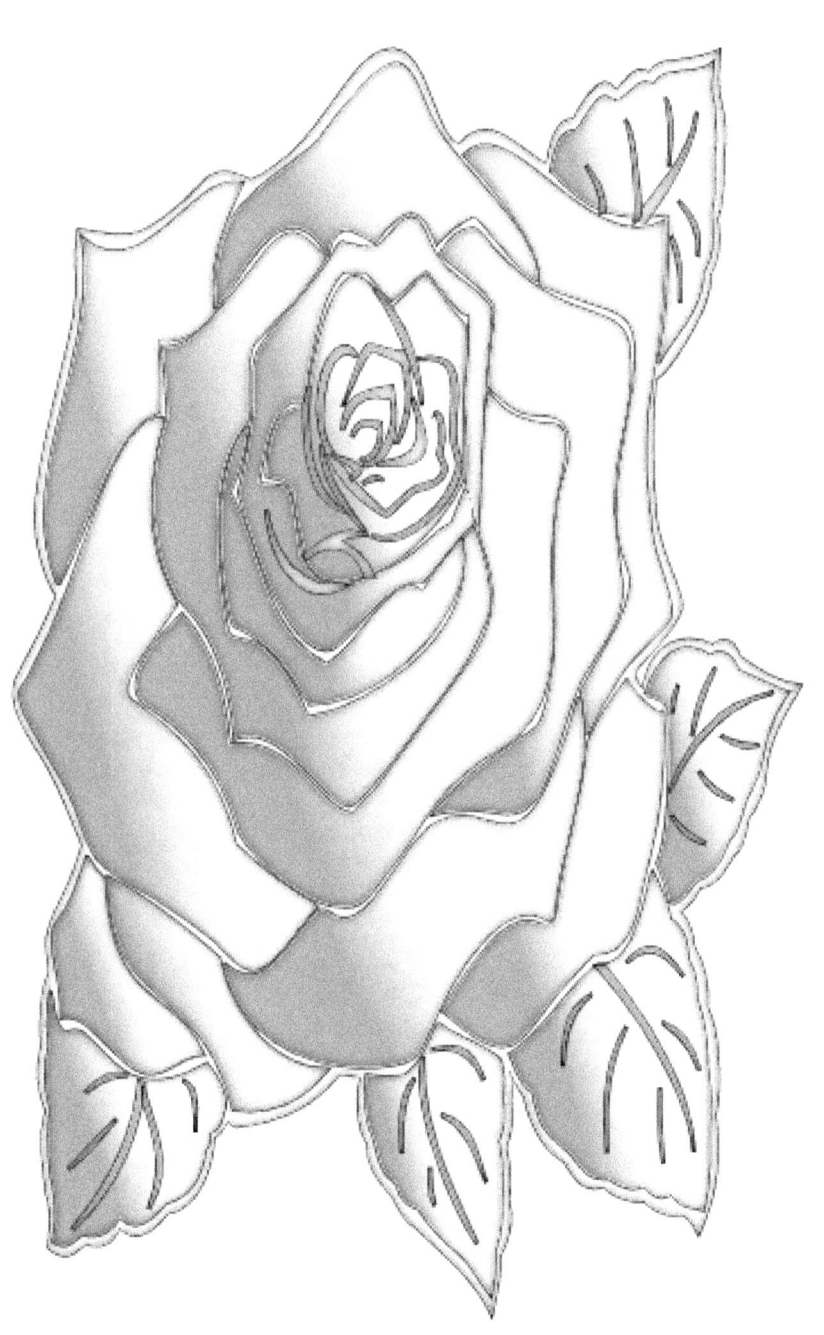

Leaves with Flower

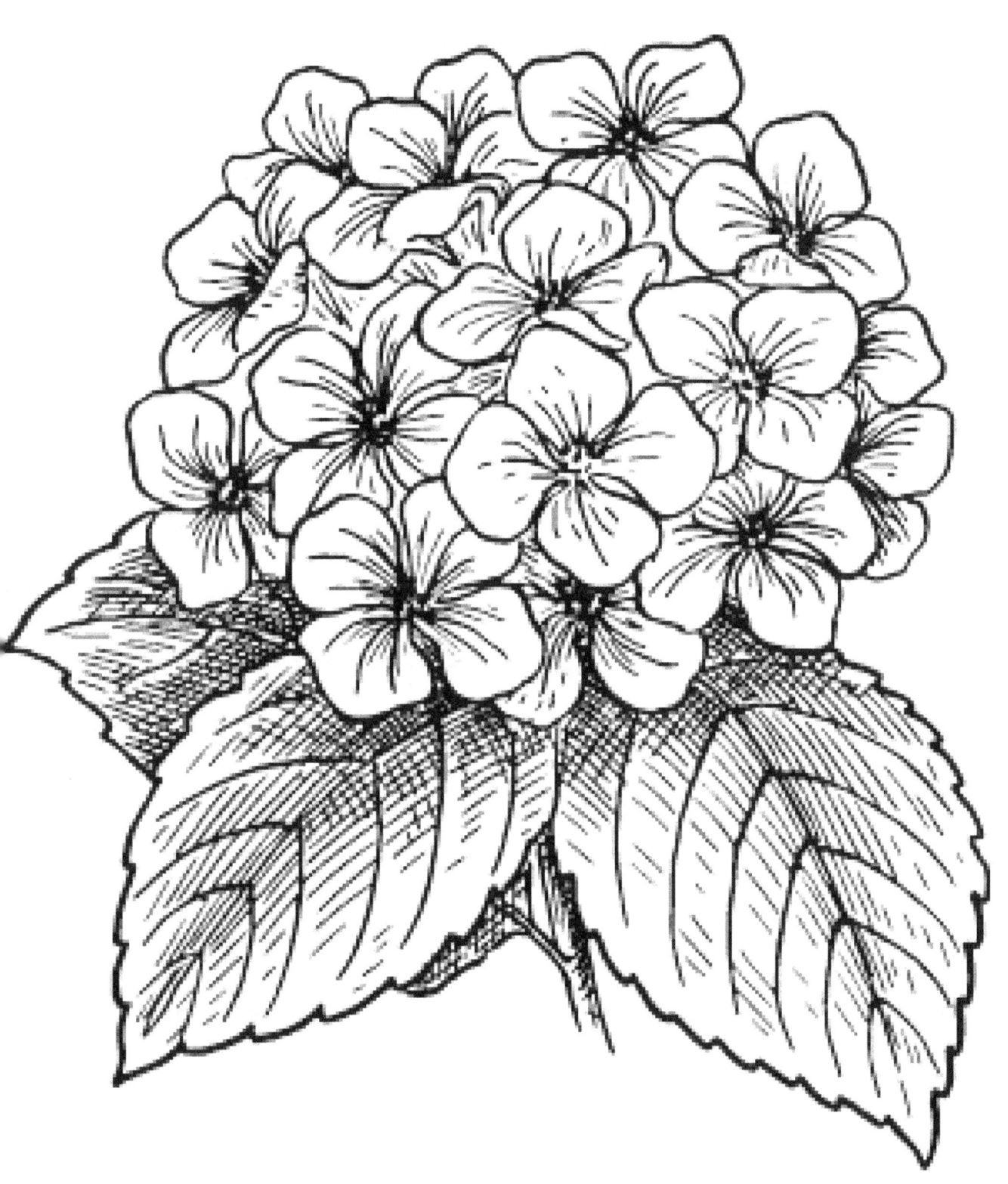

Floral mandala

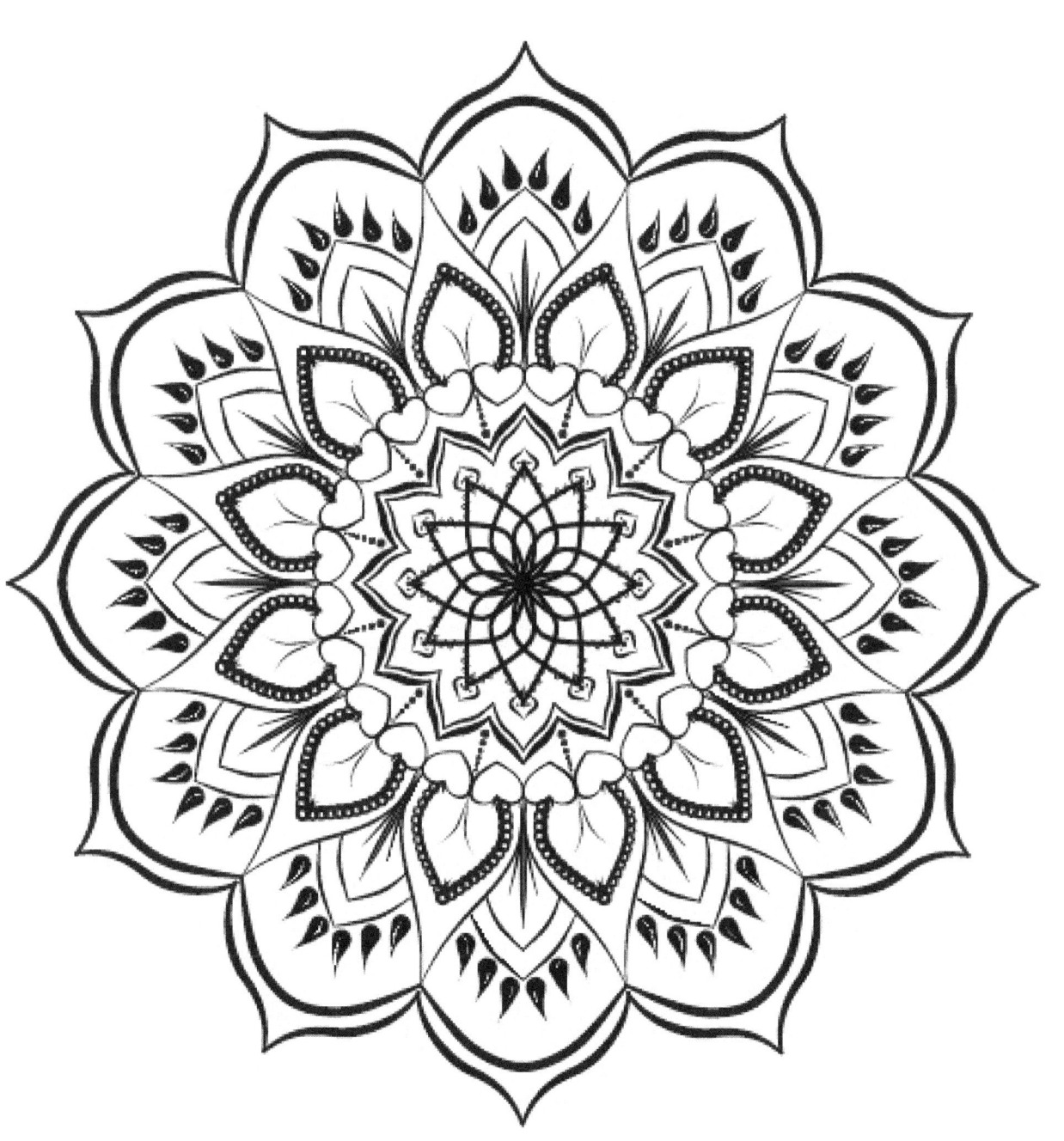

Leaf with flower

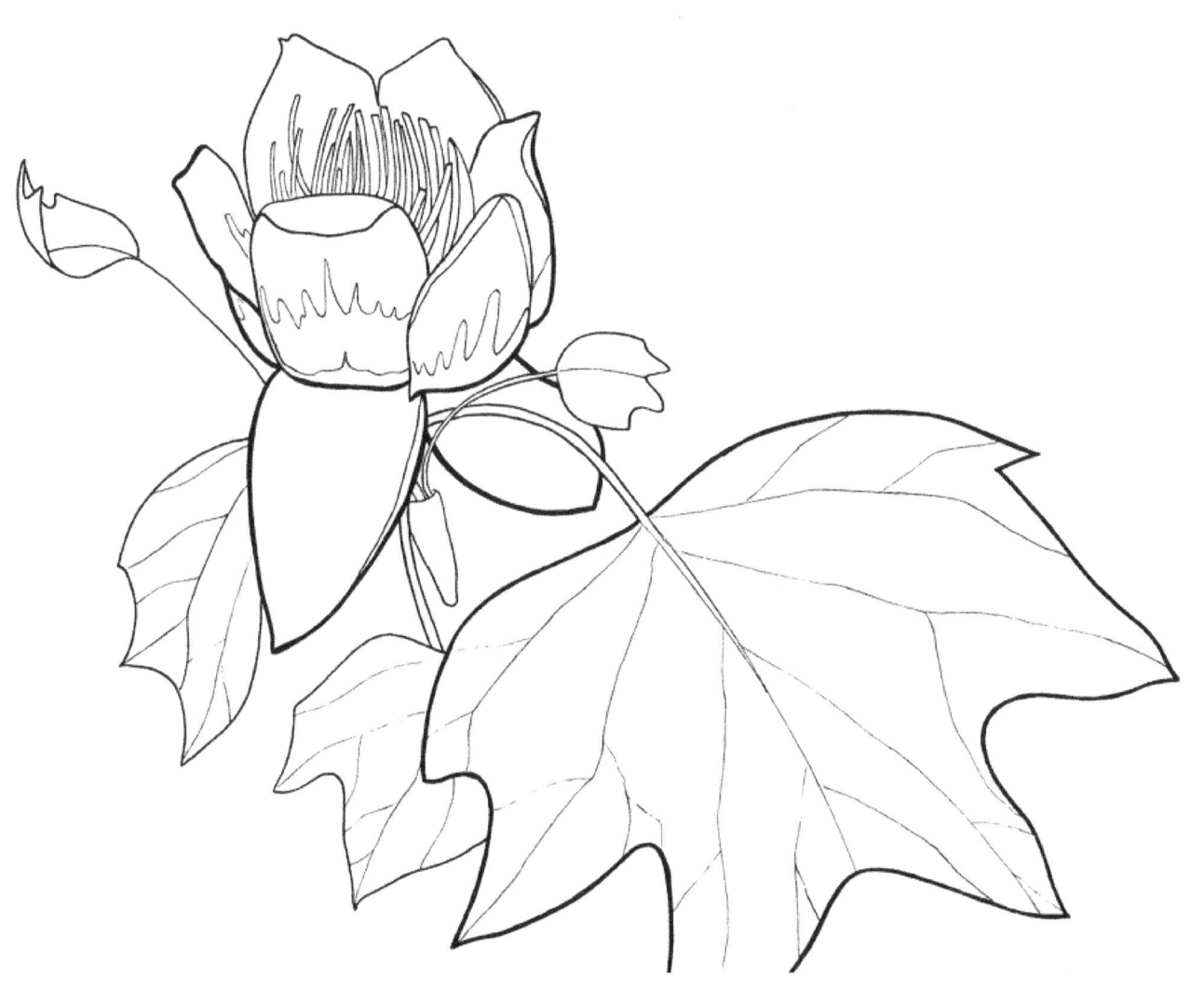

Blooming Flower

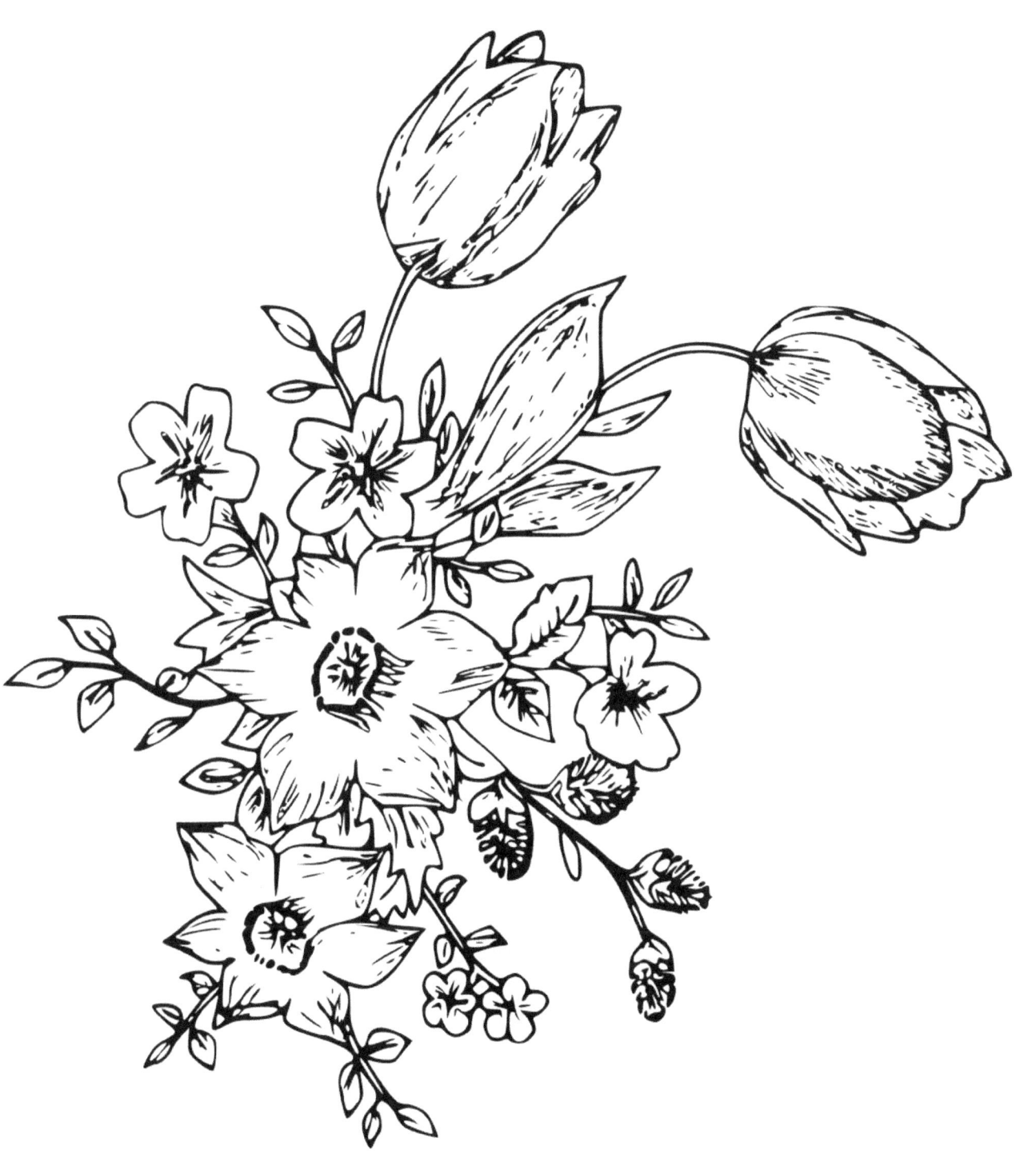

Charming Flower

Hibiscus

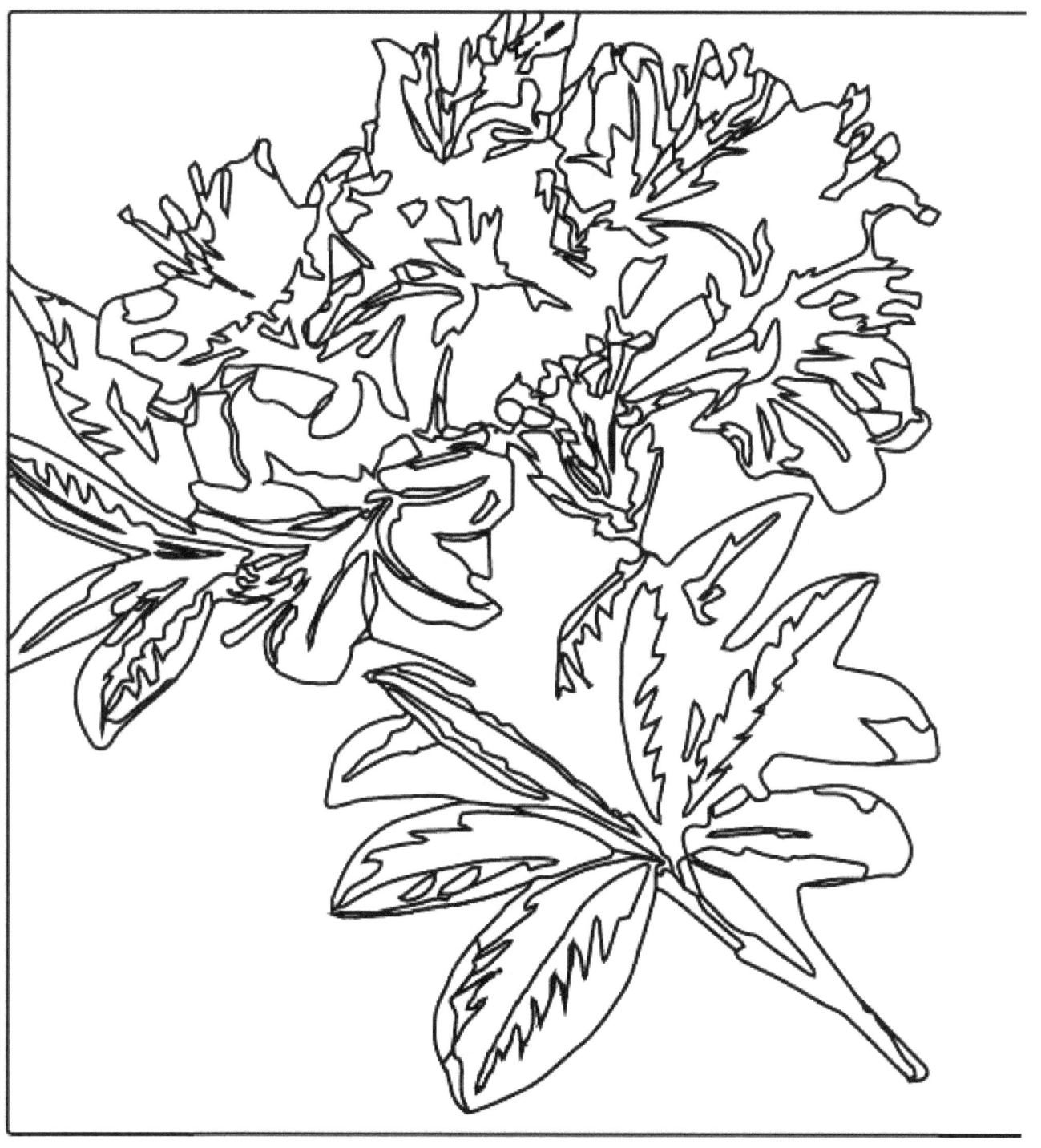

Flower Buds

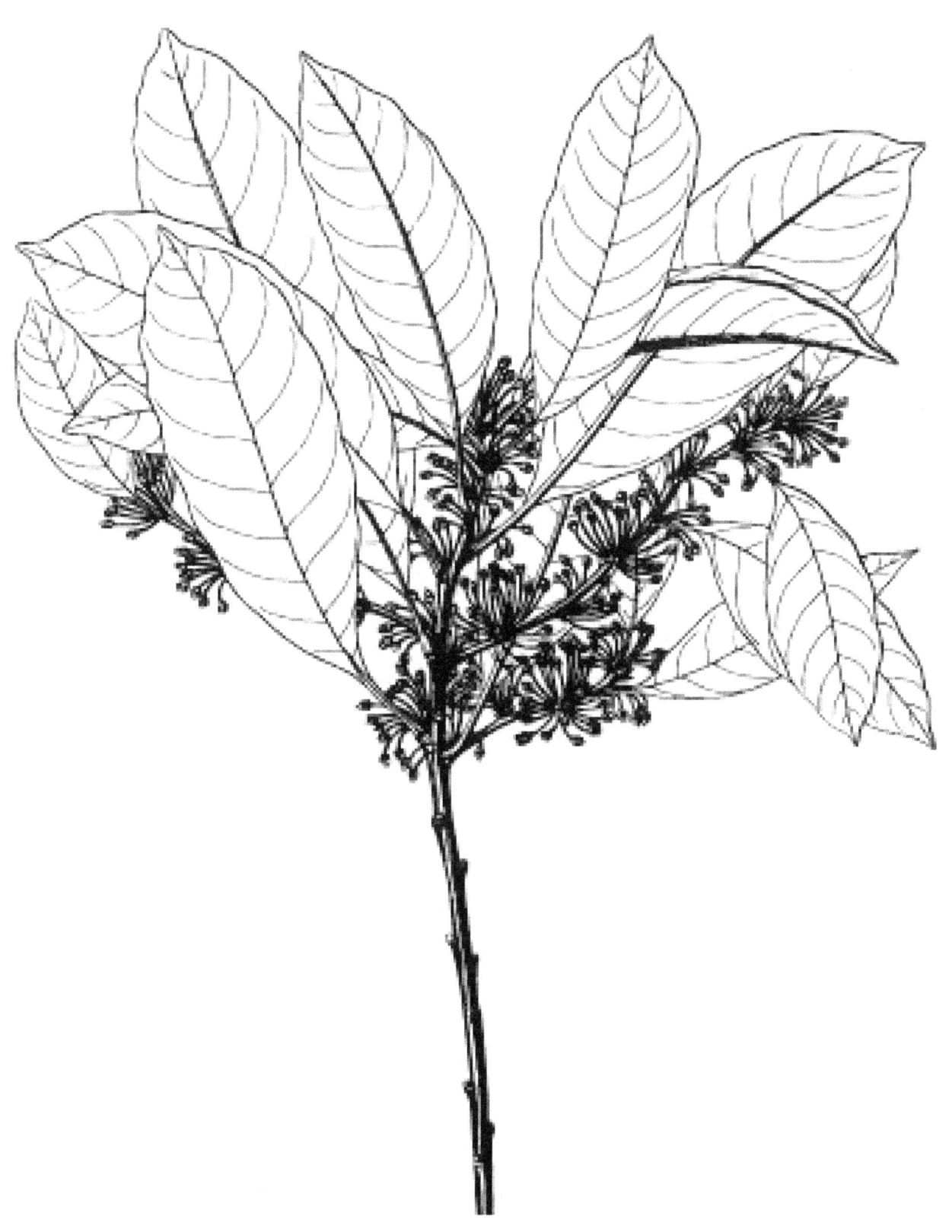

Blooming Rose

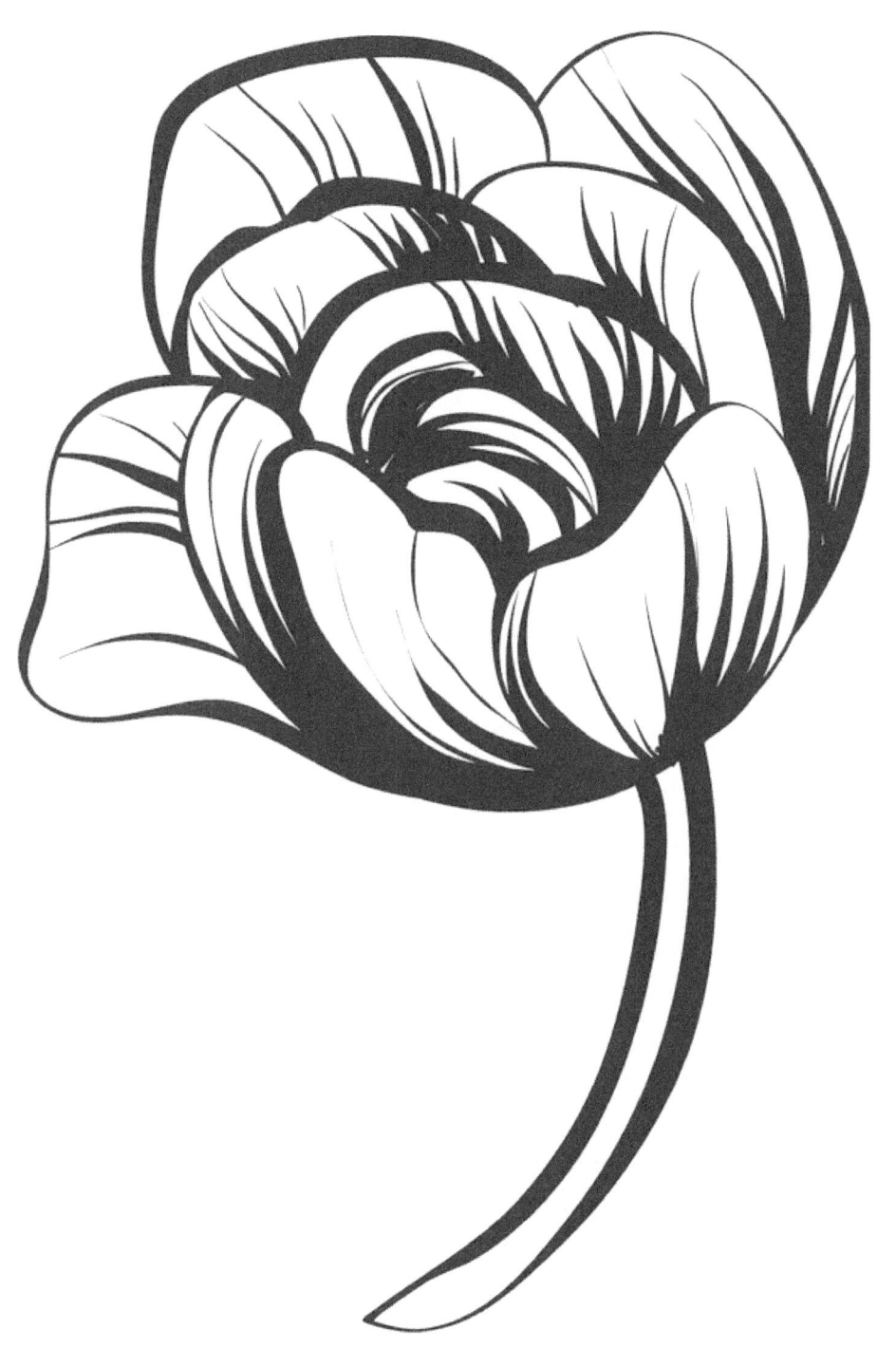

Rose Buds

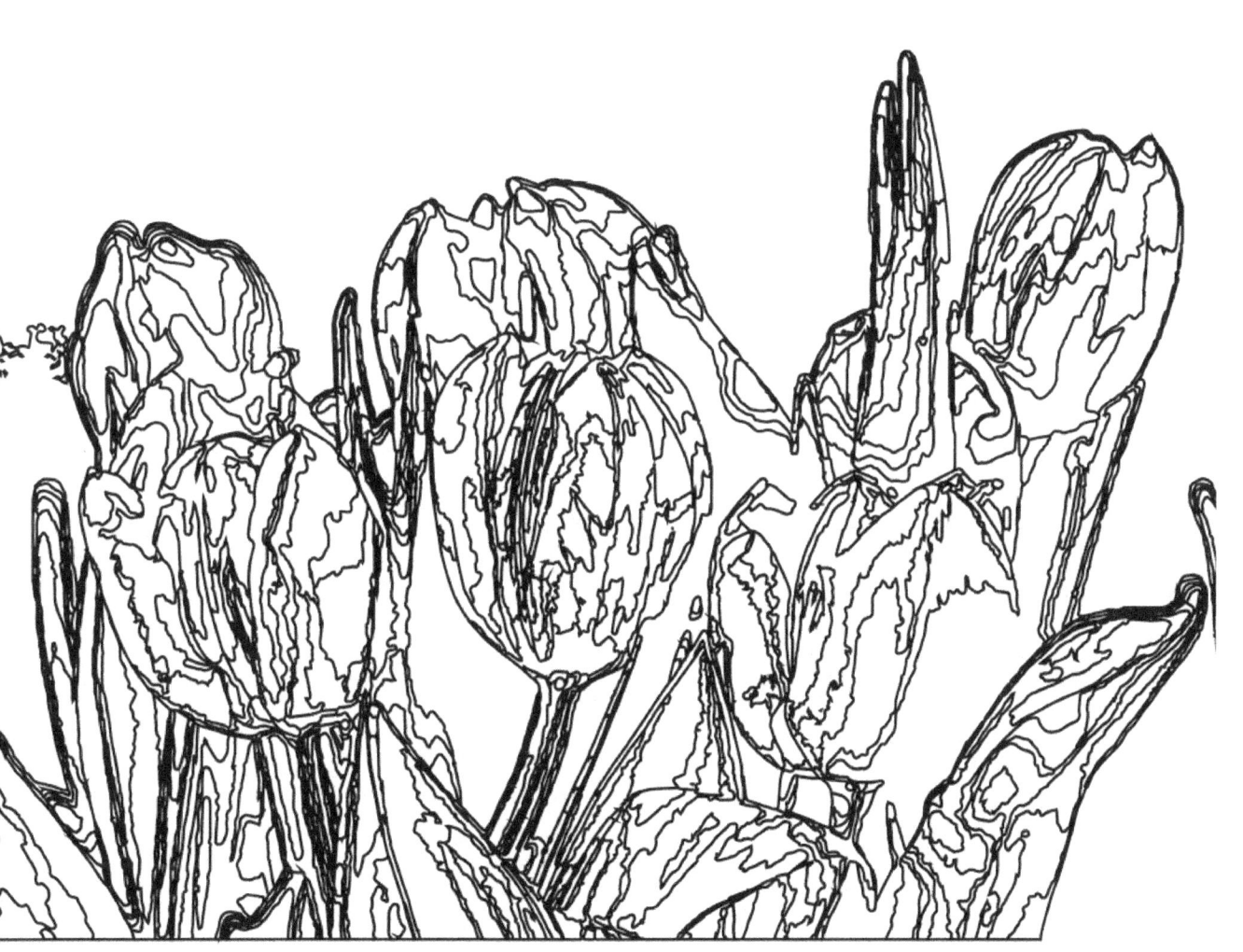

Dahlia

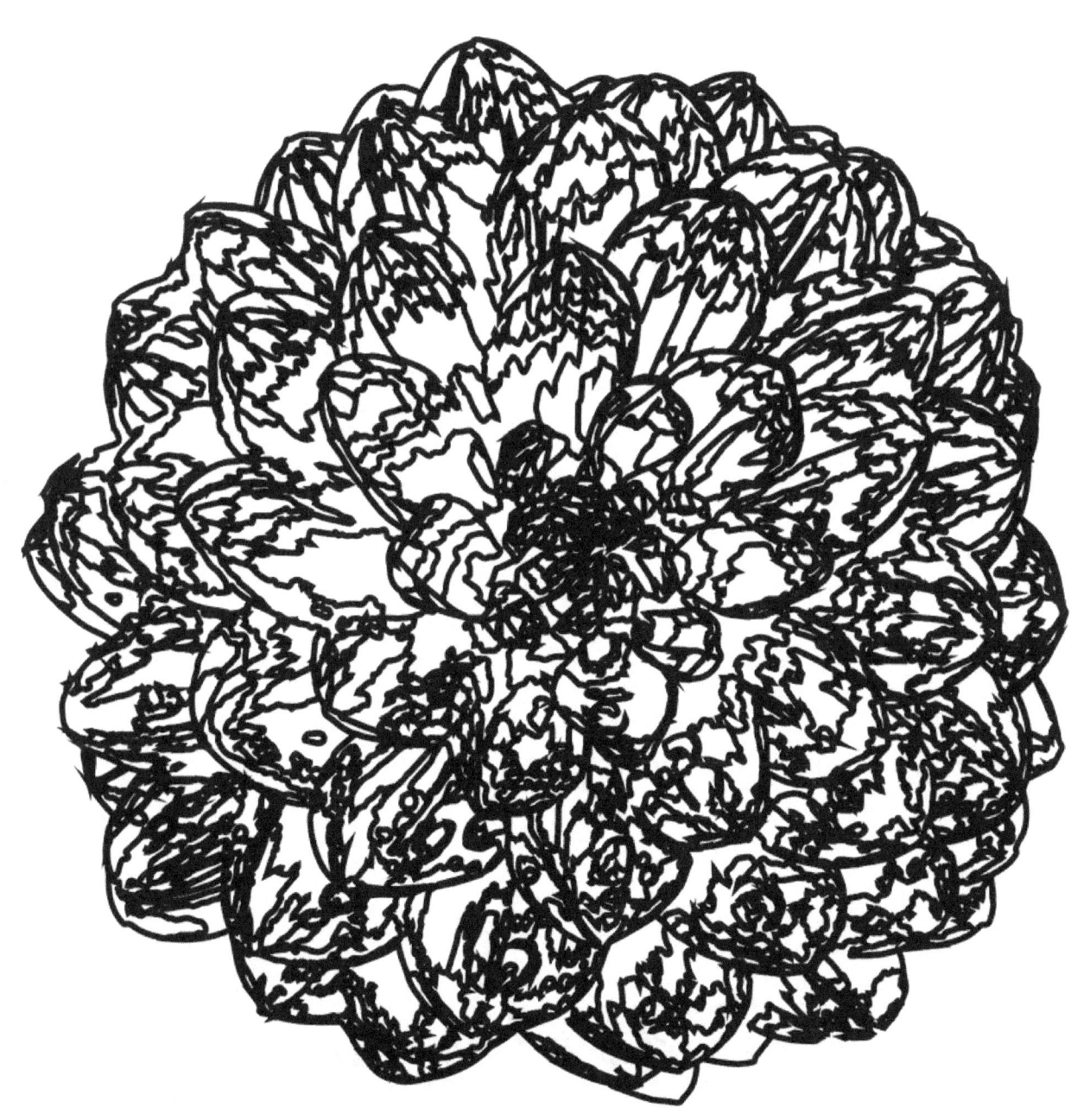

Mind-blowing Flower

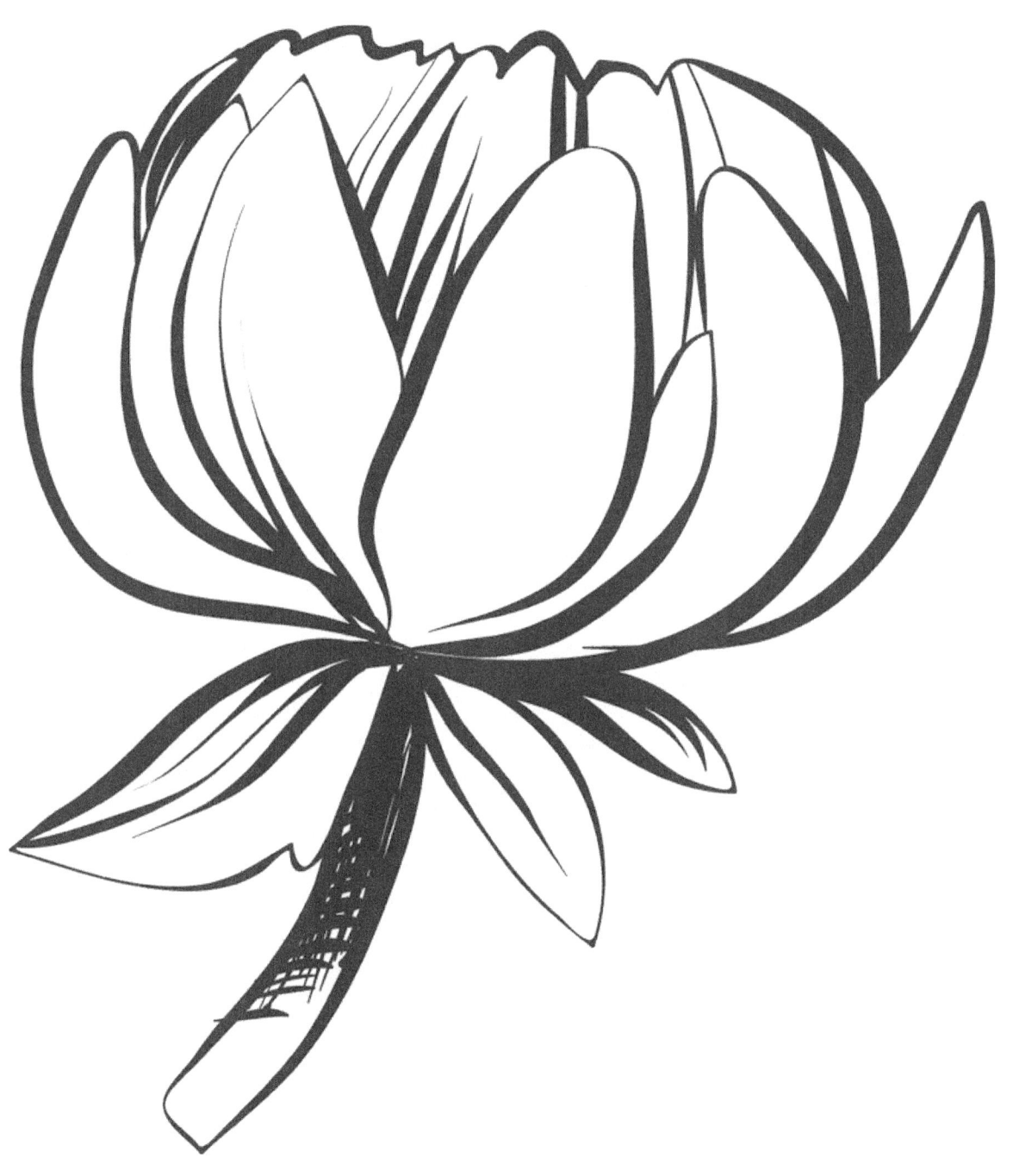

Flower Buds

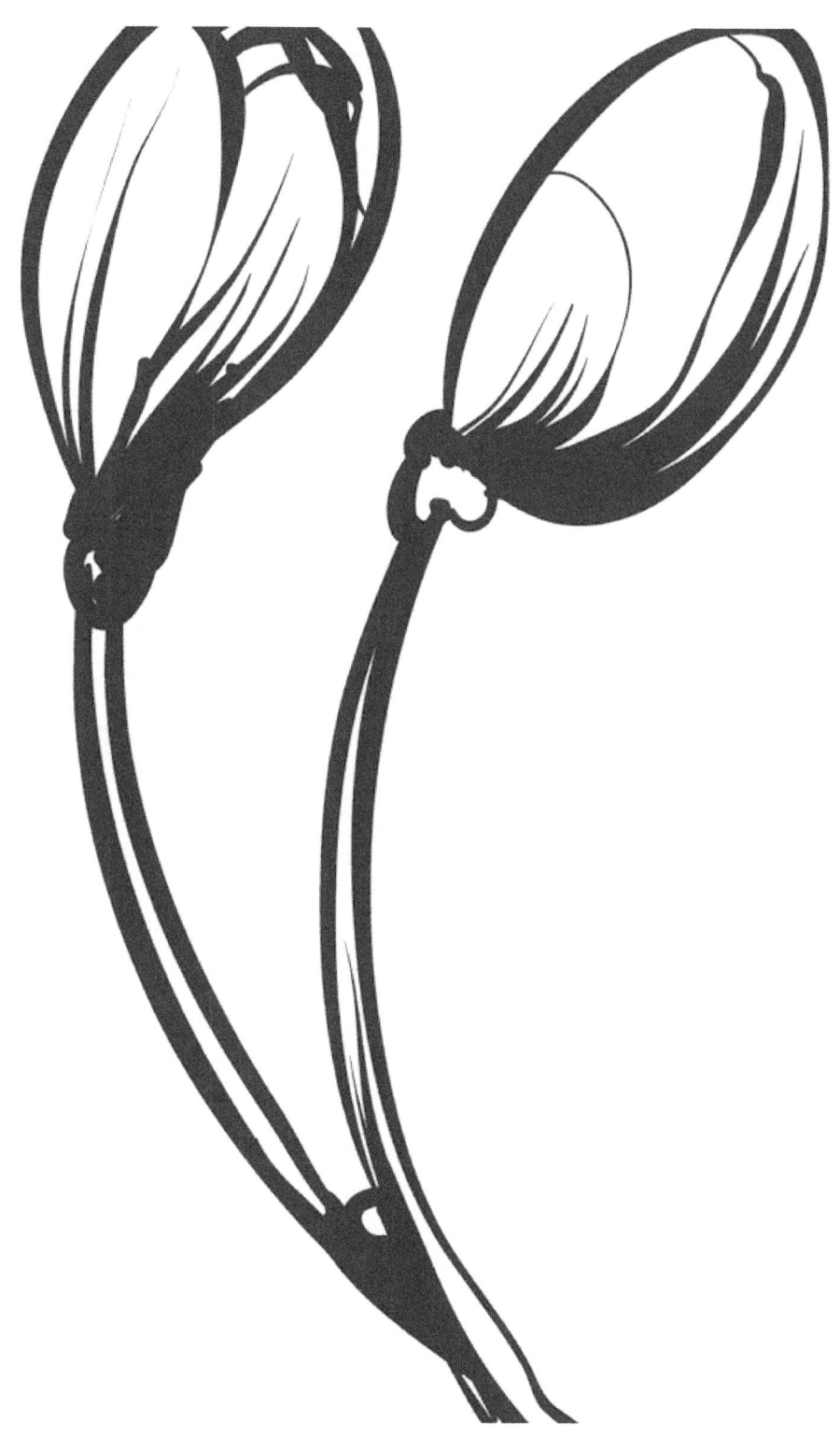

www.ingramcontent.com/pod-product-compliance
Lightning Source LLC
Chambersburg PA
CBHW080628220526
45467CB00011B/3423